The Hail Mary

Hail Mary, full of grace!
The Lord is with thee;
blessed art thou among women,
and blessed is the fruit of thy womb,
Jesus.
Holy Mary,
Mother of God,
pray for us sinners,
now and at the hour of our death.
Amen.

Glory Be to the Father

Glory be to the Father,
and to the Son,
and to the Holy Spirit;
as it was in the beginning,
is now,
and ever shall be,
world without end.
Amen.

Grace at Meals

Bless us, O Lord,
and these your gifts,
which we are about to receive from your bounty,
through Christ our Lord.
Amen.

Prayer to Our Guardian Angel

Dear Angel of God, my Guardian dear,
to whom God's love entrusts me here
ever this day be at my side
to watch and guard,
to rule and guide.
Amen.

Presented to

_____

From

_____

Date

_____

Catholic Book
of Bible Stories

Written by Laurie Lazzaro Knowlton
Illustrated by Doris Ettlinger

ZONDERKIDZ

Catholic Book of Bible Stories
Copyright © 2003 by Laurie Lazzaro Knowlton
Illustrations© 2003 by Doris Ettlinger
Requests for information should be addressed to:
Zonderkidz, *3900 Sparks Dr. SE, Grand Rapids, Michigan 49546*

ISBN 978-0-310-70505-5

Imprimatur for Catholic Book of Bible Stories

Nihil Obstat	**Imprimatur**
†Rev. Charles R. Dautremont, S.T.L.	†Most Rev. Robert J. Rose, D.D.
Censor Deputatus	Bishop of Grand Rapids
September 1, 2003	September 3, 2003

Note: The *nihil obstat* and *imprimatur* are official declarations that a book or pamphlet is free of doctrinal and moral error. No implication is contained therein that those who have granted the *nihil obstat* and *imprimatur* agree with the contents, opinions, or statements expressed.

Library of Congress Cataloging-in-Publication Data

Knowlton, Laurie Lazzaro.
  Catholic book of Bible stories / by Laurie Lazzaro Knowlton ; illustrations by Doris Ettlinger.
    p. cm.
    Summary: A collection of over fifty stories from the Old and New Testaments, each followed by a "Faith to Grow" note to reinforce the key points from a Catholic perspective, a hands-on activity to reinforce the story's theme, and a prayer.
    ISBN 0-310-70505-3
    1. Bible stories, English. 2. Catholic Church——Doctrines——Juvenile literature. [1. Bible stories. 2. Catholic Church——Doctrines.]
I. Ettlinger, Doris, ill. II. Title.
BS551.3.K56 2004
220.9'505--dc22

                                            2003015629

Project Management and Editorial: Catherine DeVries
Art direction and design: Jody Langley
Interior composition: Susan Ambs

17 18 19 20 /ASC/ 18 17 16 15

Dear Friends,

As a young mother, I wanted to share with my family my relationship with Jesus Christ. Just as the little children of the scripture sought a personal relationship with Christ, I wanted my children to know him as a loving father with open arms.

My three-year-old daughter had a natural hunger to discover Jesus. She wanted to know more about this "Lord" we prayed to nightly. And so I went on a journey of sorts, seeking out ways to make the Word a reality to her. I spent many hours pouring over scripture, trying to find ways to make the text child-friendly. I wanted my children to know the joy of being part of God's family.

What I came to realize is that life is not perceived through only one sense: the sense of hearing. God gave us five senses to experience the world, and five senses to experience him.

With this in mind, the editor, designer, and I worked hard to create a beautiful, well-told book of Bible stories. The stories are short and have been simplified for easy understanding. And I wanted to leave plenty of room for a faith response. I felt it was important for the adult and child to discuss the stories and relate them to today. Extending that one step further, I felt it was imperative to teach the child that prayer is open communication with God.

At the back of this book, I have added short, simple, engaging activities to help your faith journey include all five of your senses. It is my heartfelt desire that you and your child will use this book as the beginning of a great relationship built on the joyful experience of spending time together. I wish you blessings. May you build many fine memories.

Sincerely,

Laurie Sazzano Knowlton

Contents

God's Wonderful Creation

Genesis 1–2

In the very beginning of time, God decided to create the world. On the first day of creation, God separated light from darkness. "I will call the light 'day' and the darkness 'night,'" God said.

On the second day, God said, "I will divide the waters." He separated the sky above from the world below.

On the third day, God saw the earth covered with water. "This earth needs dry land." He rolled back the waters so that some dry ground appeared. God said, "I will make plants and towering trees." Evening came to God's third day.

"I must have a source of light for the day and night," God said. So he rolled up a ball of warm colors and formed a sun. God scattered the night with sparkling stars and a bright moon. This was a beautiful fourth day.

On day five, God sprinkled the seas with colorful, swimming fish. The gentle breeze sang the songs of birds in flight. God loved his creation.

On day six, God said, "I will create all sorts of animals to fill my earth." So he created lions, giraffes, elephants, and frogs. Bunnies hopped, kitties meowed, and dogs barked bow-wow!

"Something is still missing," God said. From the earth he made a man and then a woman. "I give you all that you see," he told them. "Take care of my creation. Be good to each other. Fill your home with children and happiness." God watched the sun set on the sixth day.

When the sun rose on the seventh day, God declared, "Today is a day of rest!" And he smiled at all he had created.

God's Blessing

God created the world.

Faith to Grow

God created everything on this earth, and
then he asked people to take care
of his creation.

Prayer

Thank you for creating the world, Lord.
Your creation is beautiful!
In the name of the Father, and
of the Son, and of the Holy Spirit.
Amen.

Adam and Eve Disobey God

Genesis 2–3

Remember what day God created the first man and woman? It was on day six. Adam and Eve did everything together. They were very happy.

But Satan, God's enemy, could not stand God's perfect world. "I must do something!" Satan decided. So he made himself look like a snake and wrapped himself around the branch of the tree of wisdom. Satan stuck out his forked tongue to smell the ripe fruit from the beautiful tree.

"Simply scrumptious!" the snake hissed.

Eve heard the snake and asked, "What is scrumptious?"

The snake answered, "This fruit."

"That is the fruit from the tree of wisdom," said Eve. "God has said we can't eat from that tree. If we do, we will die."

"No! You won't die. God is afraid you will gain the knowledge of good and evil. You will be like God."

Eve wanted to eat some, even though God had told her and Adam not to. So she took a bite. "Mmm," she said.

Adam saw that Eve didn't die when she ate the fruit. She offered him some, and Adam took a bite. Suddenly, Adam and Eve realized they were naked. They ran and hid in the bushes.

Then God called to Adam and Eve. They did not answer. But God knew where they were. "Why are you hiding from me?" he asked.

"We didn't want you to see us naked," Adam answered.

"You have eaten from the forbidden tree!" God said. "I love you both, but you may not live in my garden anymore." It was a very sad day for everyone.

God's Blessing

God loves us, even when we make mistakes.

Faith to Grow

Adam and Eve chose to disobey God.
And they no longer could live in
God's beautiful garden. But God still
loved Adam and Eve even though
they disobeyed him.

Prayer

Lord God, thank you for forgiving
me and loving me, even when I make
mistakes. In the name of the Father,
and of the Son, and of the Holy Spirit.
Amen.

Noah's Faithful Journey

Genesis 6:9 — 9:17

God saw that many of his people were sinning. They were stubborn, crabby, and mean. They didn't take good care of each other or the earth. They did things that God hated.

So God thought, "I'm sorry I created people. I'm going to wash them away and make the earth a good place again." God was ready to make a flood, but then he saw that Noah was still obeying him and doing good things. God smiled.

"Noah," God said. "I am sending a flood to wipe out everything that is bad. So I want you to make a really large boat—an ark. Build it big enough to hold two of every kind of animal. Make room for food. Then bring your family and climb aboard."

Noah obeyed God. Clip-clop, thump-thump, boing-boing—all the animals went into the ark. And so did Noah and his family. When everything was done as God commanded, God shut the door of the boat.

Outside, the rain poured down. The waters rose high, and the ark rocked back and forth. Only Noah, his family, and the animals on the ark were left.

Finally, God stopped the rain and sent a breeze to dry the earth.

Noah sent a raven to find dry land. The raven didn't find dry land, so it came back to the ark. Then Noah sent out a dove. The dove came back, too. Noah waited seven days, and then he sent out another dove. That dove returned with an olive leaf in its beak!

"The land is almost dry!" Noah said.

God said, "You all may leave the ark now."

Noah and his family left the ark. Noah built an altar. He thanked God and praised him. "Thank you, God, for saving us."

God was pleased with Noah and all he had done. "Never again will I destroy people and animals with a flood," he said. "As a sign of my promise, I will give you a rainbow. Go and enjoy this new world."

God's Blessing

God saved Noah and the animals from the flood.

Faith to Grow

Noah never questioned God. He obeyed
God. Noah trusted God to take care of
him. God provided a second chance for
people and for the animals, too.

Prayer

Thank you for showing your mercy on
Noah and the animals, Lord, and to us still
today. In the name of the Father, and of
the Son, and of the Holy Spirit.
Amen.

God's Promise to Abraham

Genesis 12:1–8; 18:10–14; 21:1–7

After Noah and his family left the ark, they had children, and their children grew up and had children. Soon there were many people living on the earth again, including Abram and Sarai. They were happy and comfortable living in the country of Haran.

One day God came to Abram and said, "Leave your family and friends and go to a place I will show you. I will bless you with a large family, and you will always be remembered."

Abram gathered all of his livestock, his wife, and his nephew Lot. They said good-bye to everyone they knew. After they had traveled for some time, they came to the land of Canaan. The Lord appeared to Abram and said, "This is the land I will give your future family."

Abram was so happy that he built God an altar. Abram praised God because Canaan was so beautiful.

God was pleased with Abram and decided he would give him the name Abraham, meaning "the father of nations," for that's what he would be someday. God also told Abraham that Sarai would now be called Sarah.

God watched over Abraham and Sarah. One day the Lord appeared to Abraham and said, "When I return to you next year, you and Sarah will have a son."

Sarah laughed when she heard the news. "How can an old woman have a baby?" she asked.

God asked Abraham, "Why does Sarah laugh? Is anything too hard for me to do?"

Sure enough, the Lord did as he promised, and one year later Abraham and Sarah had a beautiful baby boy. They named him Isaac.

God's Blessing

God keeps his promises.

Faith to Grow

God made a promise to Abraham:
"Go where I tell you and I will bless
you and your family." Abraham left
everything he knew and trusted
God's plan for his life.

Prayer

Lord, help me trust you as Abraham did.
In the name of the Father, and of
the Son, and of the Holy Spirit.
Amen.

God Remembers Joseph

Genesis 37–46

Joseph was Jacob's favorite son. Jacob made Joseph a beautiful robe to wear. It was a robe made of many different colors. Joseph's brothers were jealous.

"Let's get rid of him," the brothers said. One day they caught Joseph, threw him into a pit, and then sold him as a slave. The brothers lied and told their father, "Joseph has been eaten by wild animals." Jacob's heart was broken. How could Joseph's brothers betray Joseph like that?

But God was with Joseph. Even as a slave, Joseph was treated well by his master. Later, the master's wife lied about Joseph and Joseph was thrown into jail.

Again, God was with Joseph. The jailer liked Joseph. He put Joseph in charge of the prisoners.

One night two prisoners had bad dreams. With God's help, Joseph explained the dreams. Not long after, the pharaoh had a bad dream. He said, "Bring Joseph to explain my dream."

Joseph said, "With God's help, I will tell you the meaning of your dream." Joseph told the pharaoh that the dream was a warning. "There will be seven years of good times and seven years of very bad times," he said.

The pharaoh saw that God was with Joseph. Pharaoh said, "Joseph, you are now in charge of taking care of my land."

During the good years, Joseph was wise and put away plenty of food so that when the bad times came, Joseph was able to save the people from going hungry.

Joseph's brothers were hungry. When they went to Pharaoh to get help, they met their long-lost brother. They didn't know it was Joseph because he was all grown up now. But Joseph recognized them and told them who he was.

The brothers remembered the terrible thing they had done to Joseph as a young boy. They trembled in their sandals, afraid that Joseph would hurt them.

But Joseph said, "I forgive you. I know that it was God's plan for me to come here and save all the people from going hungry. I am glad to have my family again."

God's Blessing

God is with us, no matter what happens.

Faith to Grow

Many bad things happened to Joseph.
His brothers sold him into slavery.
He was put in prison. His friends forgot
about him. But through it all, God
was with him, turning the bad things
into something good.

Prayer

Thank you, Lord, that you are
always with me no matter what.
In the name of the Father, and of
the Son, and of the Holy Spirit.
Amen.

God Watches Over Baby Moses

Exodus 2

Joseph's brothers moved to Egypt, and their families grew larger and larger. They were God's people, the Hebrews. They had many children, and their children had many children. The new pharaoh made the Hebrews work very hard. He was cruel to them. But God was with the Hebrew people, and the families continued to grow.

"There are too many of these Hebrew people!" the mean pharaoh said. "Kill all the baby boys!"

The Hebrew people were frightened and cried out to God.

A Hebrew woman had a baby boy. She loved him very much and hid him from Pharaoh. "Please, God, help me save my son," she prayed.

When the woman couldn't hide her baby anymore, she made a basket and covered it with tar so that it would float. The woman placed her beautiful son in the basket and hid him in the weeds along the river.

"With God's help," she told her daughter Miriam, "watch over your brother." The baby rocked in the shallow water as Miriam watched close by. Then Moses began to cry.

Pharaoh's daughter came to the river to bathe. She saw the basket and heard the baby.

"Go and bring me that basket," she told her servant.

"Look! A baby!" said the princess. "I will take him home with me."

Miriam rushed out from her hiding place. She offered, "My mother can nurse your baby."

"Bring her to me," said Pharaoh's daughter. She rocked the baby and kissed his cheeks. "I will call him Moses, because I brought him out of the water."

Moses' mother was grateful to God for saving her son.

God's Blessing

God can save us from dangerous situations.

Faith to Grow

Moses' mother loved her son so much.
She did everything she could to protect
him. She loved him so much she was
willing to allow him to be adopted so that
he could be saved from certain death.

Prayer

Thank you for watching over me,
Lord. And thank you for the people
who love me. In the name of the Father,
and of the Son, and of the Holy Spirit.
Amen.

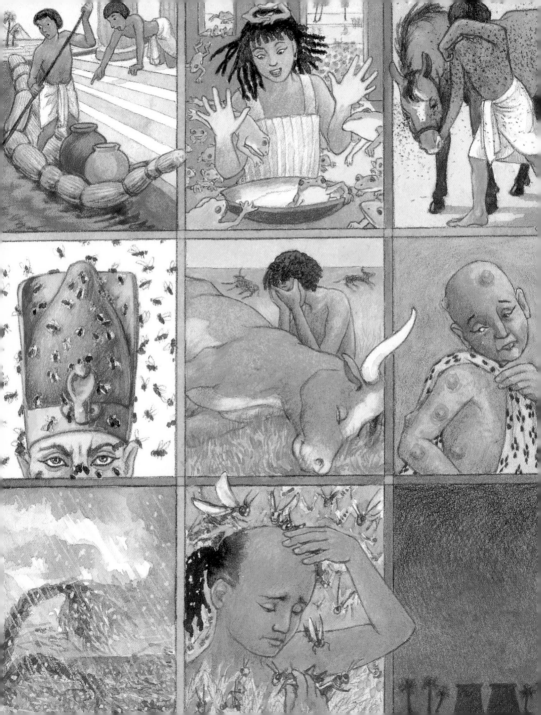

God Saves the Israelites

Exodus 3–15

God heard the Israelites cry out to him for help. God said to Moses, "Tell Pharaoh to let the Israelites go."

But Moses said, "Pharaoh won't listen to me. I am not a good speaker."

God said, "Moses, tell your brother Aaron my commands. He will talk to Pharaoh for you."

Moses and Aaron went to see Pharaoh. They told him, "God said to let the Israelites go free."

Pharaoh did not believe Moses and Aaron. He did not believe the signs that Moses performed to prove God was with him.

"Tell Pharaoh," said God, "that he will be punished if he doesn't do as I tell him."

Pharaoh would not listen to Moses and Aaron.

So God changed all the water into blood. He sent thousands of frogs, gnats, flies, sickness, and sores.

Pharaoh still wouldn't let the Israelites go. He thought, "Who will do the work if I let the Israelites go?"

God sent hail and then locusts. Still Pharaoh wouldn't let the Israelites go. So God caused an overwhelming darkness.

Finally, Pharaoh called for Moses and Aaron to come to him. "Take your people out of Egypt. But leave your animals." But that wasn't good enough.

Then God delivered the worst plague of all. "Every one of your firstborn children and first-born animals shall die," God said.

God told the Israelites to mark their doors with the blood of a sacrificial lamb so that the angel of death would pass over their homes. But the Egyptians were devastated. They cried to Pharaoh about the loss of their children and animals.

So Pharaoh told Moses, "Leave Egypt at once! Take your animals and go!" God had saved them.

God's Blessing

God saved the Israelites.

Faith to Grow

God wants all people to
know that he alone is God.

Prayer

You alone are God. Help me tell others
about you. In the name of the Father, and
of the Son, and of the Holy Spirit.
Amen.

Crossing the Sea

Exodus 13:17 — 14:31

The Israelites who left Egypt had always been slaves. Their food came from Pharaoh. But now they would have to learn to take care of themselves and depend on God. They were tired, hungry, and scared. They complained loudly.

"Moses, did you bring us out of Egypt to let us die in the desert?" they asked. But still they followed Moses to the edge of the Red Sea.

"Look! Pharaoh has followed us!" cried the frightened Israelites. "He has come to take us back to slavery." The desert sands whipped around them.

God spoke to Moses and said, "Lift your staff over the water and the Red Sea will part."

The sea parted, and the Israelites escaped through the dry path in the middle of all the water. The Egyptians followed the Israelites through the sea, but the waters crashed down on them.

God had saved the Israelites once again!

Moses and his people celebrated getting to the other side of the Red Sea. They were happy. They sang about their freedom. They sang about their mighty God.

God's Blessing

God can do anything!

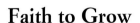

Faith to Grow

God is able to do anything,
even part the sea. Nothing is
impossible for God.

Prayer

Dear God, you are so powerful.
You can do anything!
In the name of the Father, and of the Son,
and of the Holy Spirit.
Amen.

God Provides
Bread from Heaven

Exodus 16

Moses and the Israelites walked day after day through the desert. They were tired and afraid. "We are running out of food!" they complained. "Moses, did you bring us out of Egypt to starve?"

God heard the Israelites grumbling. God said, "Moses, tell the people that in the evening they will eat meat and in the morning they will eat bread as sweet as honey. By this, the Israelites will know the glory of God."

In the evening a huge flock of quail flew into the camp. The women cooked them up like chicken. And the next morning, the ground was covered with fine white flakes.

When the Israelites saw the flakes, they asked Moses, "What is this?"

"This is the bread that the Lord has given you," said Moses. "Take and eat it." They called the flakes manna.

The Israelites ate the quail in the evenings and the sweet bread of manna during the day. Every day each family gathered enough manna to eat that day. On the sixth day of every week, they gathered extra manna for the Sabbath. They rested on the seventh day, praising God for his goodness.

For forty years the Israelites ate God's special food.

God's Blessing

God gives us everything we need.

Faith to Grow

God provided the Israelites with
everything they needed. He gave them
a special kind of bread called manna.
God still provides us with special
bread during Eucharist.

Prayer

Thank you, God, for always providing
for our needs. In the name of the Father,
and of the Son, and of the Holy Spirit.
Amen.

Rules to Live By

Exodus 20:1–17

Moses and the Israelites wandered in the desert. The people began doing whatever they liked. They didn't have any rules to live by. God told Moses to meet him on top of a mountain. There, God gave Moses a set of rules for his people to follow. These rules are called the Ten Commandments. After Moses left the mountain, he shared God's rules with the people.

Moses told them, "The most important rule is to love and worship God." He also told them:

Do not worship other gods.

Never use God's name in a bad or angry way.

Always remember to keep one day each week special for God.

Treat your parents with respect.

Do not kill another human being.

Do not take another person's husband or wife for yourself.

Never take things that don't belong to you.

Do not say unkind things about other people.

It is not good to want what other people have.

Now Moses and his people knew how to live a life that would honor God and keep them from hurting themselves and other people.

God's Blessing

God gave us rules to live by.

Faith to Grow

God shows us how to live a godly
life by loving him and treating other
people as we would like to be treated.

Prayer

Lord God, thank you for showing me how
I should live. Most of all, help me to be
like Jesus, loving others as much as I love
myself. In the name of the Father, and of
the Son, and of the Holy Spirit.
Amen.

God Gives Samson Strength
Judges 13–16

After the Israelites spent forty years in the desert, they were allowed to go into Canaan, which they called the promised land. But they needed leaders to guide them. So God sent them judges. One of these judges was Samson. He was born to serve God. God gave Samson a gift.

"Samson, you are special," God said. "I'll give you a gift of great strength. The secret is that your strength will leave you if you cut your hair."

Samson kept his secret and grew to be stronger than a lion. Samson was even stronger than a thousand men. Samson had enemies who wanted to know his secret.

Samson fell in love with Delilah. His enemies bribed Delilah. They said, "If you find out the secret to Samson's strength, we will give you a lot of money."

Delilah asked Samson to tell her the secret of his strength. Samson made up a reason. Delilah said, "You tricked me! If you really loved me, you would tell me."

Samson knew it was wrong to tell Delilah his secret, so he tricked her again.

Delilah complained, "How can you say you love me when you won't tell me your secret?"

Samson loved Delilah, even though she didn't love God. Samson forgot his promise to God. He told Delilah his secret. Delilah said, "Now I know you truly love me. Come and rest."

Samson fell asleep. And Delilah broke his trust. She told Samson's enemies to cut his hair. He became weak. Samson's enemies tied him up, hurt him, and put him in jail.

But God remembered his promise to Samson. Samson's hair began to grow while he was a slave.

His enemies said, "Bring Samson to the temple. We will make fun of him and his God." They brought Samson to the temple and tied him between two columns.

Samson called out to God, "Deliver me from my enemy. Strengthen me again so that I can show my enemy your mighty power."

Samson's power returned. He pushed the temple columns down, destroying the temple and everyone inside.

God's Blessing

God gives us gifts to use for his glory.

Faith to Grow

As long as Samson followed
God's ways, God made
Samson very strong.

Prayer

Thank you for blessing me with a gift,
Lord. Help me to know what it is.
In the name of the Father, and of
the Son, and of the Holy Spirit.
Amen.

The Lord Calls Samuel

1 Samuel 3

Hannah wanted to have a baby. She prayed to God at the temple. She was crying because she wanted a baby so badly. The priest saw her. When he understood why she was crying, he blessed her and wished her well. God answered Hannah's prayer. She was so thankful. She sent Samuel to work in the temple.

One night in the temple, Samuel heard someone call his name. He sat up and rubbed his eyes. He thought Eli the priest had called him, so he ran to Eli. "Here I am," Samuel said.

Eli said, "I did not call you. Go back to bed."

A while later, Samuel heard his name being called again. He ran to Eli and said, "Here I am."

Eli shook his head. "I did not call you. Go back to sleep."

A third time Samuel heard his name called! He ran to Eli again. "Here I am."

Eli finally understood. He said, "God is calling you, Samuel. Go to sleep. When you hear your name being called, answer, 'Your servant is listening.'"

That's exactly what Samuel did, and God talked to Samuel. Samuel listened.

Samuel shared what God said to him with the people. And Samuel did God's work the rest of his life.

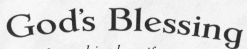

God's Blessing

God lets us know his plans if we listen for him.

Faith to Grow

God called Samuel. Samuel listened.
And Samuel did God's work.

Prayer

Help me to listen for you, Lord.
In the name of the Father, and
of the Son, and of the Holy Spirit.
Amen.

David and Goliath

1 Samuel 17

The Israelites were at war with the Philistines. The Philistines didn't want to give up their land, which God had promised to the Israelites.

The Philistines chose their most frightening warrior to challenge the Israelites. Goliath was a giant of a man. He was over nine feet tall!

"Send one of your men to fight me!" Goliath roared. "The one man who wins the fight will win the war."

There wasn't a single Israelite who had the courage to fight Goliath. Every morning and every night for forty days, Goliath dared God's people to fight him. But the Israelites were scared.

David, a young shepherd boy, came to the Israelites' camp to visit his older brothers. He heard Goliath making fun of the Israelites and their God.

"I will fight Goliath!" cried David.

Everyone said, "You are just a boy. You can't beat Goliath."

David said, "Goliath depends on his own strength. But God is my strength." He knew he could defeat the giant with God's help.

King Saul offered David his royal armor for protection. But it was too heavy for a boy. David said, "I don't need armor. God is my protector."

Then brave David chose five small stones, put them in his bag, and held his slingshot in hand. Goliath laughed and laughed when he saw David. "I called for a warrior, and they sent me a boy!"

David said to Goliath, "You come to fight me with armor and a sword. I come against you with God Almighty. You will lose this battle."

Then David pulled a stone from his bag, loaded his slingshot, and fired. Goliath fell to the ground—and died.

David said, "Today the world will know that the God of Israel is almighty."

God's Blessing

God helps us to be brave.

Faith to Grow

Goliath depended on his own strength,
and lost. David depended on God to be
his strength, and won.

Prayer

Help me to be brave like David and trust
in you, God. In the name of the Father,
and of the Son, and of the Holy Spirit.
Amen.

Solomon Asks for Wisdom

1 Kings 3:5–15

When David grew up, he became a great king over the Israelites. God loved him very much. David had a son named Solomon. Like David, Solomon loved God and obeyed his laws.

One night God appeared to Solomon when he was fast asleep in the palace. God said, "Ask something of me, and I will give it to you."

Solomon answered, "God, you have blessed me. You have given me thousands of people to rule. Lord, grant me the wisdom to judge my people fairly. Help me to see right from wrong."

"I am pleased with you, Solomon," God said. "You did not ask for selfish things like money, long life, or the death of your enemy. I will give you wisdom beyond any other. Your heart will be full of understanding; because you did not ask for wealth and fame, I will bless you with these things also. Continue to walk in my ways, and you will have a long life."

When Solomon woke up from the dream, he went to Jerusalem and worshiped God.

God's promise was true. Solomon ruled his kingdom with the wisdom of God. Solomon solved disagreements fairly. He listened to his people with understanding. He ruled his kingdom with justice. Solomon was known far and wide for being a wonderful king who loved God.

God's Blessing

God gives us wisdom.

Faith to Grow

Isn't it wonderful that God hears
our requests? Solomon didn't ask for
selfish things. Solomon asked for wisdom,
which would make him a better person.
God was pleased with Solomon.

Prayer

Lord God, help me to be wise like
Solomon. In the name of the Father,
and of the Son, and of the Holy Spirit.
Amen.

God Feeds Hungry Elijah

I Kings 17:1–16

God spoke to his people through prophets. One of his prophets was Elijah. God gave Elijah messages for the people, but the people didn't listen. Elijah was tired and discouraged. Many wicked people were after him. So Elijah ran away into the wilderness to hide.

Hard times came. There was no rain to grow crops. There was no food to eat. The Lord said to Elijah, "Go to the east. There, you will find a stream to drink from. I will send ravens to feed you."

Elijah found the stream of water just as God said. Every morning and every evening, ravens brought Elijah bread and meat. Elijah stayed there until the stream dried up.

Then God came to Elijah again and said, "Go to Zarephath. You will find a widow there. She will feed you."

Elijah walked and walked until he finally found the widow gathering sticks. He was very thirsty.

"Please bring me a small cup of water," Elijah said. The widow dropped her sticks and went to get Elijah water.

"Please bring me a bit of bread, too," Elijah called.

The widow answered, "I have nothing made. I was gathering wood to prepare bread from the last of my flour and oil. My son and I were going to eat one last time. After that, we will surely die because we are so hungry."

Elijah said, "Go and make the bread as you planned. But first give me a bite to eat. Then feed yourself and your son. My Lord promises that you shall not run out of flour or oil."

The widow did as Elijah asked. God blessed her with plenty of flour and oil, just as Elijah said. The widow and her son did not go hungry after all!

God's Blessing

God takes care of us.

Faith to Grow

God uses difficult times to show
people how to be their best. God used
the widow to show us a lesson in giving
to others. The widow chose to share
with Elijah, even though she believed
it could mean going hungry.

Prayer

Help me to always be giving.
In the name of the Father, and
of the Son, and of the Holy Spirit.
Amen.

The Lord Is my Shepherd

Psalm 23

David wrote many psalms to God. Psalms are like poems or songs. David sang many of the psalms. In this psalm, David is showing God's love and care for us. David speaks of God as a shepherd and of himself as one of the shepherd's beloved sheep.

"The LORD is my shepherd;
  I have everything I need.
  He lets me rest in fields of green grass
  and leads me to quiet pools of fresh water.
  He gives me new strength.
  He guides me in the right paths,
  as he has promised.
  Even if I go through the deepest darkness,
  I will not be afraid, LORD,
  for you are with me.
  Your shepherd's rod and staff protect me.

"You prepare a banquet for me,
where all my enemies can see me;
you welcome me as an honored guest
and fill my cup to the brim.
I know that your goodness and love
will be with me all my life;
and your house will be my home as long as I live."
(Good News Translation)

God's Blessing

God is our shepherd.

Faith to Grow

David knew God had been at his side
all of his life. God has also been with
you since before you were born.
God loves you like a father.

Prayer

Thank you, God, for loving me as a caring
father. In the name of the Father, and of
the Son, and of the Holy Spirit.
Amen.

God Knows Me

Psalm 139:1–6

In this psalm, David thought a lot about God's complete understanding about everything. He was amazed to realize God knew him. God knew where David would live, what he would do, and the very words he would speak. And God knows all this about us, too.

"Lord, you have examined me and you know me.

You know everything I do;

from far away you understand all my thoughts.

You see me, whether I am working or resting;

you know all my actions.

Even before I speak,

you already know what I will say.

"You are all around me on every side;

you protect me with your power.

Your knowledge of me is too deep;

it is beyond my understanding."

           (Good News Translation)

God's Blessing

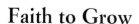

God knows us completely.

Faith to Grow

God knows everything.
He knows you and loves you
just as you are.

Prayer

Thank you for loving me just as I am.
In the name of the Father, and of the Son,
and of the Holy Spirit.
Amen.

Praise God!

Psalm 150

Psalm 150 is a psalm of great celebration. The writer encourages the reader to use his voice and a band of instruments to praise God.

"Praise the LORD!

Praise God in his Temple!

Praise his strength in heaven!

Praise him for the mighty things he has done.

Praise his supreme greatness.

Praise him with trumpets.

Praise him with harps and lyres.

Praise him with drums and dancing.

"Praise him with harps and flutes.

Praise him with cymbals.

Praise him with loud cymbals.

Praise the LORD, all living creatures!

Praise the LORD!"

(Good News Translation)

God's Blessing

God loves it when we praise him!

Faith to Grow

Praising God should be a joyful
celebration. Sometimes we forget to praise
God for his majesty. Isn't it great to know
God loves to hear us praise him?

Prayer

I will praise God with all my heart, body,
and soul! In the name of the Father, and of
the Son, and of the Holy Spirit.
Amen.

Isaiah the Prophet Brings Hope

Isaiah 40

The Israelites had suffered a long, long time. "Where is our God?" they cried. God saw the Israelites' misery and sent words of comfort, through the prophet Isaiah.

He said, "Do not be afraid, Israel, because you have paid for your sins. You are now forgiven."

"Shout to the world the good news! Tell everyone your God is coming!

"He is coming to rule the world with power. He will bring along with him the people he has rescued. He will take care of his people like a shepherd takes care of his beloved flock.

Who can be compared to God?

He knows everything.

He created everything.

He sees everything.

Lift up your eyes and see your Creator! Because of his strength, not one of you is missing. He is your God forever."

"Hope in your Lord and you will not be disappointed.

Your strength will be renewed.

You will soar like an eagle!"

God's Blessing

God will never let us down.

Faith to Grow

Never give up your hope in the Lord.
He alone will be your strength
and your salvation.

Prayer

Lord, I will place my trust in you.
In the name of the Father, and
of the Son, and of the Holy Spirit.
Amen.

God Keeps Daniel Safe

Daniel 6

The Israelites ignored God's prophets who told them not to forget about God and live lives that would please him. Finally, the powerful Babylonians conquered the Israelites. Daniel, along with many of God's people, was taken as a slave to Babylon.

Daniel became a trustworthy, hardworking, godly man. He was a great prophet of God. Daniel was also King Darius' favorite servant. This made all of King Darius' other servants jealous. They wanted to get rid of Daniel.

King Darius' servants knew Daniel prayed to God every day. They said, "We will get the king to make a law against praying to God."

"King Darius, you alone are the almighty!" they said. "Make a law against worshiping anyone besides you. Then whoever breaks the law will be thrown to the lions!"

King Darius signed the new law. The king's servants waited and watched for Daniel to pray.

"King Darius!" the wicked servants said, "Daniel has broken your law! We saw him praying to his God."

King Darius was very sad. He loved Daniel. He tried to stick up for Daniel. But the mean servants said, "King Darius, you made the law unbreakable!" So King Darius had no choice. Daniel was taken to the lions' den.

"May the God you love save you," King Darius told Daniel. Daniel was thrown into the lions' den. Then the king returned home, deeply sad. He worried all night.

Early the next morning, the king rushed to the lions' den. He called, "Daniel! Has your God protected you?"

Daniel answered, "I am safe! My God sent angels to close the lions' mouths."

King Darius rejoiced. He told the whole kingdom, "Daniel's God is the living God. He is a deliverer and a Savior!"

God's Blessing

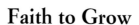

God protects us.

Faith to Grow

God is our protector.
He loves us. He cares for us.
He wants to protect us from harm.

Prayer

Thank you for protecting me
and for loving me, Lord.
In the name of the Father,
and of the Son, and of the Holy Spirit.
Amen.

Jonah and the Big Fish

Jonah 1–4

Jonah was another prophet. His job was to give people messages from God. God told Jonah, "Go to Nineveh. Tell the people to behave. They are breaking my laws."

Jonah didn't want to do what God said. He knew that Nineveh was a bad place. The whole city was evil. He ran away and found a boat sailing away from Nineveh. "I will hide from God on this ship," he thought.

But God saw Jonah. He was angry Jonah hadn't done what he asked. He sent a terrible storm to toss the ship.

The sailors cried, "What have we done to anger the gods?"

Jonah told them, "You haven't done anything. This storm is my fault. I made the One True God very angry. I tried to run away from him. I didn't want to do what he asked me to do."

"What shall we do?" asked the sailors.

"Throw me overboard," said Jonah. "Then you will be safe."

The sailors threw Jonah into the fierce waves. The sea was instantly calm. The men saw how strong and powerful Jonah's God was, and they worshiped him.

God sent a big fish to swallow Jonah. For three days and nights Jonah sat in the belly of the great fish. He had a lot of time to think about what he had done. He prayed to God for forgiveness.

God forgave Jonah. He commanded the fish to spit Jonah out on the shore. Again, God said, "Tell the people of Nineveh to change their ways."

Jonah went straight to Nineveh and warned the people of Nineveh. They were sorry for breaking God's Laws. God forgave them.

God's Blessing

God is forgiving.

Faith to Grow

Our God is a forgiving God. He will
punish us when we need to be punished,
but he loves us even when we sin. God
gives us a second chance to listen to him.

Prayer

Help me listen to you, Lord.
Help me do what you want me to do.
In the name of the Father, and
of the Son, and of the Holy Spirit.
Amen.

The Annunciation

Luke 1:26–38

A long time after Jonah, God sent the angel Gabriel to Nazareth to a virgin named Mary. Mary was engaged to Joseph, who was from the house of David. "Peace be with you! The Lord is with you and has greatly blessed you!" said Gabriel.

Mary was surprised and afraid. "Don't be afraid, Mary," said Gabriel. "God has been gracious to you." Mary wondered what the angel's words meant.

"You are going to have a son," said Gabriel. "And you shall call him Jesus. He will be called the Son of the Most High God, and his kingdom shall last forever."

Mary couldn't help but wonder, "How can this happen? I am not yet married."

The angel Gabriel said, "The Holy Spirit will come to you, and God's power will rest upon you. For this reason the holy child will be called the Son of God. Your old cousin Elizabeth is also going to have a son. Nothing is impossible for God."

Trusting God, Mary replied, "I am the Lord's servant. May it happen to me as you have said."

God's Blessing

God uses us to do great things if we trust in him.

Faith to Grow

Mary was a faithful, trusting
servant of God. She said yes to God.

Prayer

Help me to have faith like Mary and trust
you as she did. In the name of the Father,
and of the Son, and of the Holy Spirit.
Amen.

The Birth of Christ

Luke 2:1–20

Mary and Joseph of Nazareth had promised to marry each other. Mary was going to have a baby. Caesar Augustus ordered the Jewish people to go to the town where their ancestors had come from. Caesar wanted to know how many people there were so they could pay him money, called a tax.

Joseph and Mary traveled to Bethlehem, the city of Joseph's ancestor, David. When they arrived, they couldn't find a place to stay. An innkeeper felt sorry for Joseph and Mary and offered them his stable. That night, Mary gave birth to her baby son. She wrapped him in cloth and placed him in a manger filled with soft hay.

An angel of the Lord appeared to shepherds in the fields and announced, "We have good news! Today in Bethlehem the Savior has been born. You will find him wrapped in cloth and sleeping in a manger." Then all the angels burst into songs of praise.

The shepherds said, "Let us go see what has happened!" They found Mary and Joseph, and they saw

the baby lying in the manger. "We saw angels, and they told us the good news! Today our Savior is born."

Mary looked upon her baby boy with love.

God's Blessing

God gave us his Son to save us from our sins.

Faith to Grow

When baby Jesus was born, he needed to
be loved and cared for by his mother. He
got hungry and sleepy, just as all babies do.
Jesus became a human being, like you and
me, so that he could save us.

Prayer

Thank you for sending Jesus as
our Savior. In the name of the Father,
and of the Son, and of the Holy Spirit.
Amen.

The Wise Men Visit Jesus

Matthew 2:1–15

Wise Men from the East, who studied the stars, followed one very bright star to Jerusalem. They went to King Herod and asked, "Where is the newborn king of the Jews?"

King Herod didn't know about Jesus' birth. He called all of his priests and scribes together and asked, "Where is the Savior to be born?"

The priests and scribes answered, "The prophets say he is to be born in Bethlehem of Judea."

Herod told the Wise Men, "Go to Bethlehem and search for the child. Send for me when you find him. I want to go and honor him, too."

The Wise Men left Jerusalem. Again, the star they had followed rose and moved across the sky ahead of them. It led them to where Jesus was with his mother, Mary.

The Wise Men bowed down and honored Jesus. They gave him magnificent treasures of gold, frankincense, and myrrh, which were symbols of his being our

King and Savior. When they left, the Wise Men were warned in a dream not to return to Herod because Herod wanted to harm Jesus.

Joseph also had a dream. An angel told him, "Leave for Egypt tonight! Herod is afraid of Jesus and wants to kill him." So Joseph took Mary and Jesus to Egypt where they stayed until Herod died.

God's Blessing

Jesus is the Messiah.

Faith to Grow

God had big plans for Jesus. The Wise Men knew that the prophets foretold the coming Messiah. God sent his only Son so that our sins could be forgiven and we could live forever in heaven.

Prayer

Help me to be wise like the Wise Men, who came to worship the Savior. In the name of the Father, and of the Son, and of the Holy Spirit. Amen.

Jesus in His Father's House

Luke 2:41–52

When Jesus was twelve years old, his family and relatives traveled to Jerusalem as they did each year during the Feast of Passover. When the feast was over, Jesus' family and relatives gathered and began their journey home.

Jesus remained in Jerusalem without his parents' knowing. After some time Mary and Joseph realized Jesus was not among the relatives. Frightened, Mary and Joseph returned to Jerusalem to look for Jesus.

For three days they searched the streets of Jerusalem. Finally, they found Jesus in the temple. He was listening and speaking with the teachers. All who heard Jesus were amazed at his understanding of God's Word.

Mary said, "Jesus, we have been so worried! Why did you stay here?"

Jesus looked at his mother and said, "Didn't you know I needed to be in my Father's house?"

Mary and Joseph did not understand Jesus' words.

Jesus returned with Joseph and Mary to Nazareth. He obeyed them. Jesus grew smarter, stronger, and wiser, and was given favor before God. Mary thought about all these things and kept them in her heart like a treasure.

God's Blessing

Even as a boy, Jesus taught others about God.

Faith to Grow

What is a church? It is God's house.
Church is where you can learn about
God with your family, friends, and
teachers. In order to grow closer to God,
Jesus knew he needed to listen to his
teachers and other wise people who
knew about God. He wanted to learn
everything he could about God.

Prayer

Help me want to learn like Jesus.
In the name of the Father, and
of the Son, and of the Holy Spirit.
Amen.

The Baptism of Jesus

Matthew 3

Jesus had a cousin named John who lived in the desert. John wore animal skins. When he was hungry, he ate bugs and honey. God had a special job for John. God said, "You will be my messenger. Tell the people to get ready for God to come to earth."

So John preached loudly to the people. He said, "You need to be sorry for your sins! Start obeying God's laws!"

Many people came from the cities and villages to hear John speak about the Messiah, the Savior who was coming. The people knew John spoke the truth. They said, "We are sorry for our sins."

Then John baptized the people in the Jordan River. He said, "I have baptized you with water. He will baptize you with the Holy Spirit."

The people celebrated being washed clean of their sins. They were now members of God's family.

One day Jesus came to John at the Jordan River. John did not feel worthy to baptize Jesus. "I need to be

baptized by *you*. Why are you coming to *me*?" John said this
because Jesus had never sinned.

Jesus explained, "This is what God wants us to do."

Like the other people, Jesus went into the water, and John
baptized him. Then a great light shone from the sky. The Holy
Spirit came down on Jesus like a dove. A voice from heaven
said, "This is my own dear Son, with whom I am pleased."

God's Blessing

God can wash us clean from our sins.

Faith to Grow

Baptism is a celebration of joining
God's family. When you were baptized,
the priest poured holy water over your
head and anointed you with oil. You
were dressed in white clothes as a sign of
being washed clean of sin. And you
were welcomed into God's family.

Prayer

Thank you for welcoming us into
your family, Lord, through the sacrament
of baptism. In the name of the Father,
and of the Son, and of the Holy Spirit.
Amen.

Jesus Is Tempted

Matthew 4:1–11

After Jesus was baptized, the Holy Spirit led him into the desert. Jesus didn't eat anything for forty days and forty nights. He was very hungry.

The devil came to Jesus and said, "If you are God's Son, order these stones to turn into bread."

Jesus said, "Human beings cannot live on bread alone, but need every word that God speaks."

Then the devil took Jesus to the top of the temple in the holy city of Jerusalem and said, "If you are God's Son, jump! For the Scripture says, 'God will give orders to his angels about you; they will hold you up with their hands...'"

Jesus answered him, saying, "But the scripture also says, 'Do not put the Lord your God to the test.'"

Then the devil took Jesus to the top of a very high mountain and showed him the gold and jewels and power of all the kingdoms on the earth. But there was one catch. The devil told Jesus he could have it all, but first, Jesus would have to kneel down and worship the devil.

"No!" Jesus said, "Go away, Satan! The scripture says, 'Worship the Lord your God and serve only him!'"

Defeated, the devil finally left Jesus alone. Then angels came to take care of Jesus.

God's Blessing

Saying God's Word helps us fight temptation.

Faith to Grow

In the Garden of Eden, Adam and Eve
gave in to temptation and said yes to the
devil. But Jesus showed us that we can
resist the devil's temptation. Jesus said no!

Prayer

Dear God, help me to say no
to temptation as Jesus did. In the
name of the Father, and of the Son,
and of the Holy Spirit.
Amen.

Jesus Calls His Disciples

Luke 5:1–11

Jesus was teaching a crowd of people by the lake. The people drew closer and closer to him until there was no more room. Jesus saw several fishermen washing their nets by their boats.

"Simon," said Jesus, "please take me out in your boat a little way so that I can continue to teach the crowd."

Simon Peter dropped his nets and pushed his boat out into the water. Jesus continued to talk to the people from the boat. The people sat on the beach listening to Jesus' teaching. Then Jesus said to Simon, "Push the boat out further to the deep water, and let down your nets for a catch."

"Master," Simon answered, "we worked hard all night long and caught nothing. But if you say so, I will let down the nets."

Out in the deep waters, the nets quickly filled with thousands of squirming, splashing, wiggly fish. "Come and help me!" Simon yelled, signaling his friends. Soon both boats were overflowing with fish.

Simon fell on his knees before Jesus and said, "Go away from me, Lord. I am a sinful man!"

Jesus said to Simon, "Don't be afraid. From now on you will be catching people."

Returning to shore, Simon and his friends, James and John, left everything and followed Jesus.

God's Blessing

Trust in Jesus—God will provide for you.

Faith to Grow

Simon, James, and John were Jesus' first
followers. They gave up everything to
follow Jesus and his teachings.

Prayer

Dear Father, help me to follow you.
In the name of the Father, and
of the Son, and of the Holy Spirit.
Amen.

Why Worry?

Matthew 6:25–34

One day Jesus spoke to the people and said, "Don't worry! God wants you to be happy!"

Jesus pointed to the birds chirping around him. "The birds of the sky do not worry about where their next meal will come from. God takes care of them just as he will take care of you."

Jesus pointed to the flowers. "Look how God has clothed the flowers in the fields. Not even King Solomon looked as beautiful as these. God has provided for them and he will also make sure *you* get what you need."

"Why don't you have more faith?" asked Jesus. "Do not worry about what you will eat, drink, or wear. Your heavenly Father knows you need these things. Instead," Jesus said, "Spend your time and your energy working at following God's ways. Love God and follow his rules. Then God will provide for all your needs."

Jesus finished his sermon by saying, "So do not worry about tomorrow; it will have enough worries of its own. There is no need to add to the troubles each day brings."

God's Blessing

We never need to worry.

Faith to Grow

Jesus does not want us to worry.
He wants us to spend our time thinking
about and doing things that please God.

Prayer

Please help me remember not
to worry, Lord. In the name of the Father,
and of the Son, and of the Holy Spirit.
Amen.

The Faith of
the Centurion

Matthew 8:5–13

Jesus went to the city of Capernaum. A military officer, called a centurion, came to Jesus and begged for help: "Sir, my servant is sick in bed at home, unable to move. He is suffering terribly."

Jesus said, "I will go make him well."

The centurion said, "I do not deserve to have you come into my house. Just give the order, and my servant will get well." The centurion said he knew Jesus could do this because, as an officer, if he gave an order, his soldiers obeyed. If he told his slaves to do something, they did it. He knew Jesus also has that power.

Jesus was amazed because the centurion's faith was so strong. He said, "This man has shown more faith than anyone else in all of Israel." The centurion was not Jewish. He was a Gentile. Jesus wanted all people to believe in him, no matter who they were. He was very pleased with this Gentile for having such strong faith.

Jesus turned to the centurion and said, "Because you believed, your servant is healed."

When the centurion returned home, he found his servant healthy and happy.

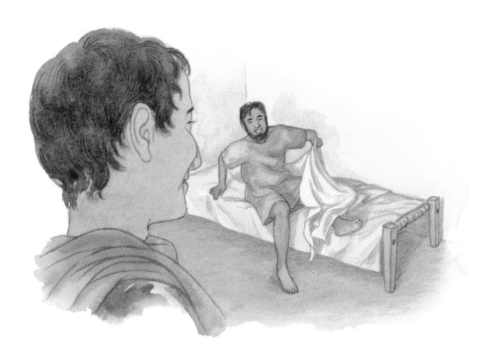

God's Blessing

God shows us his mercy and love.

Faith to Grow

We believe that if we ask for God's mercy, he will heal us of our sins. During Mass, right before Communion, we express our simple faith in Jesus, just like the centurion did. Even though we're not worthy, we tell the Lord, "Only say the word and *I* will be healed." If we ask for God's mercy, he will heal us of our sins.

Prayer

Thank you for loving me and caring about me. Help my faith in you to keep growing. In the name of the Father, and of the Son, and of the Holy Spirit. Amen.

Jairus' Daughter

Mark 5:21–43

Jesus climbed off a boat, and a large crowd gathered as he stood on the shoreline. A synagogue official named Jairus made his way through the crowd and fell at Jesus' feet.

"My daughter is dying," said Jairus. "Please come and heal her."

Jesus quickly walked with the man to his home. The crowd followed close behind them. A family member of Jairus ran up to them and said, "You are too late. She has died."

Jesus turned to Jairus and said, "Do not give up on your daughter. Have faith."

When they arrived at Jairus' home, the family gathered around weeping.

Jesus said, "Why are you crying? The child is sleeping."

The relatives made fun of Jesus. "Who is this man?" they asked. "Go away! We have lost our beloved child."

Jesus and his disciples, Peter, James, and John, and the girl's parents entered the girl's room.

Jesus took the girl's hand and said, "Child, get up!" The girl immediately woke up. Her parents couldn't believe their eyes. They said, "Praise be to God!" The parents took their daughter in their arms and showed the family.

"Rejoice!" they said. "Our daughter lives!"

Everyone stood in awe as Jesus quietly left.

God's Blessing

Rejoice in the miracles of Jesus.

Faith to Grow

Jesus wants us to have hope in him,
even when things seem hopeless.

Prayer

Lord, help me to always place
my hope and trust in you. In the
name of the Father, and of the Son,
and of the Holy Spirit.
Amen.

Jesus Feeds
Five Thousand
Matthew 14:13–21

Jesus went to a deserted place to be alone. But as usual, the crowds searched and found him. When Jesus saw the crowds and their needs, his heart was sad for them. He reached out and cured the sick people.

It was getting late in the day, and still the people did not want to go home. The disciples said to Jesus, "Tell the crowds to leave so they can return to the villages and get food to eat."

But Jesus said, "You feed the people."

The disciples said, "We only have five loaves of bread and two fish."

Jesus said, "Bring the food to me." The disciples did as they were told. Jesus told all the people to sit down on the grass.

Jesus took the five loaves and two fish and looked up to the heavens. He blessed the bread and broke it into pieces. He gave the pieces to the disciples. The disciples gave the food to the crowd.

It was a miracle! The small amount of food multiplied, and everyone ate until they were full. Jesus asked the disciples to gather up the remaining bread and fish. There was enough left over to fill twelve baskets.

The number of men who had eaten was about 5,000, and that wasn't counting women and children!

God's Blessing

God can do miracles!

Faith to Grow

Jesus performed miracles like curing
the sick and feeding thousands of
people. What is impossible for us
is not impossible for God.

Prayer

Thank you for doing miracles, Lord.
Nothing is too difficult for you.
In the name of the Father, and
of the Son, and of the Holy Spirit.
Amen.

"I Am the Bread of Life"

John 6:22–70

Jesus fed thousands of people, and they wanted to follow him. They searched and searched and finally found Jesus in Capernaum.

Jesus saw the people and said, "You search for me because I filled your bellies. Do not follow me to fill your stomachs. Follow me to have bread that lasts forever."

The people were puzzled. They asked, "How do we do that?"

Jesus said, "Believe in the One he sent."

They said, "Our ancestors ate manna (bread) from heaven. What sign can you do?" Jesus answered them by saying, "God has sent you the real bread of life."

"Give us this bread," said the people.

Jesus said, "I am the bread of life. If you believe in me, you will never be hungry or thirsty again."

The people were still confused. "How can this be?" they asked. "Isn't Jesus the son of Joseph and Mary?

Jesus heard the murmuring and said, "Whoever believes in me has eternal life. I am the bread of life."

This was too hard for them to understand. Some people said, "We cannot eat the flesh of a man or drink his blood." So, sadly, many of Jesus' followers left him.

Jesus turned to his twelve disciples and asked, "Do you want to leave me?"

Peter answered, "You have the words that give eternal life. We believe you are the Holy One of God."

God's Blessing

Jesus is the Bread of Life.

Faith to Grow

God sent his Son to sacrifice himself for
our sins so that we could have eternal life.
We show Jesus we believe in him when we
join together and receive Communion.

Prayer

Thank you for giving up your life
to save us, Lord. In the name
of the Father, and of the Son,
and of the Holy Spirit.
Amen.

You Are the Son of God

Matthew 16:13–20; Galatians 3

Jesus and his disciples had travelled all day. Finally, they sat down to rest. Jesus asked his disciples this question: "Who do the people say the Son of Man is?"

The disciples replied, "Some people believe the Son of Man is John the Baptist or Elijah. Others think he could be Jeremiah or one of the other prophets."

Then Jesus said, "That is what they think, but who do you say that I am?"

Simon Peter answered, "You are the Messiah, the Son of God."

Jesus said, "You are blessed because God told you this."

Jesus went on to say, "You are Peter. You are a rock, and on this rock foundation I will build my church . . . I will give you the keys of the Kingdom of heaven; what you don't allow on earth will not be allowed in heaven, and what you allow on earth will be allowed in heaven."

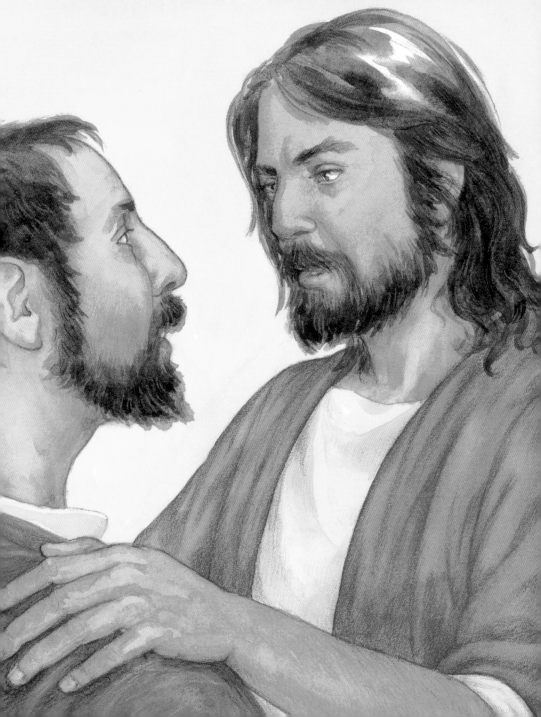

As more and more churches spread throughout the world, people became confused by what was most important. They forgot that Jesus was the Messiah and they began to think that following the Law of Moses would save them instead of Jesus. But Peter and other disciples of Jesus reminded them about Jesus, the Savior of the world.

God's Blessing

God loves us even though we aren't perfect.

Faith to Grow

Peter was not perfect, but he believed in Jesus. Jesus gave Peter the responsibility to carry on the church after Jesus died and ascended to heaven. We are not perfect either, and we too have been chosen by Jesus to become present-day saints.

Prayer

Dear Lord God, thank you for your saints. May I do your will as they did. In the name of the Father, and of the Son, and of the Holy Spirit. Amen.

The Lost and Found Sheep
Matthew 18:10–14

Thousands of people came to hear Jesus tell about God and his Kingdom. He often told parables, or stories, that would help people understand. They were simple people—farmers and shepherds and merchants. So Jesus used everyday events when he told his stories. This is one of the stories he told:

There once was a man who had one hundred sheep. One day a sheep wandered away from the rest of the flock. That was very dangerous. Bears and lions lived in the hills. The man was very worried. He didn't want to lose even one of his sheep. What should he do?

The man decided to leave the other ninety-nine and go looking for his one little lost sheep. He searched and searched. He searched up one hill and down another.

Finally, the man found his sheep. He was so happy!

"Hurray!" he said. "You were lost and now you are found!" Instead of scolding it, the shepherd led his wandering sheep back to the flock.

Jesus told this story to show us that God the Father is like the shepherd. He loves each and every one of us. We are all special to him. He does not want to lose even one of us. He never wants us to stray away from the Church, but if we do, he will come looking for us.

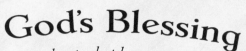

God's Blessing

God cares about what happens to each of us.

Faith to Grow

God wants all of us to belong to him.

Prayer

Help me spread the good news
about you, Lord, so that many
people may come to know you as
their Savior. In the name of the Father,
and of the Son, and of the Holy Spirit.
Amen.

To Forgive or Not to Forgive
Matthew 18:15–17

Peter went to Jesus and asked, "Lord, if a person sins against me, how many times must I forgive them?"

Jesus answered, "You must forgive them every time." Jesus then told this story:

A king was collecting from people who owed him money. He called for a servant who owed him a great deal of money. The king said, "Pay me what you owe me."

The servant was frightened. He said, "I don't have any money!"

The king said, "Then I will sell you and your family as slaves to pay your debt."

"Please! I beg you not to sell my family," said the servant. "I will pay you back."

The king had mercy, forgave the man, and forgot about his debt.

Later, the man who had been forgiven by the king met a fellow servant and said, "Give me the money you owe me!"

The servant begged for mercy, but the forgiven servant was very angry and had his fellow servant thrown in jail.

When the other servants saw this, they went to the king and told him the story. The king ordered the forgiven servant to come to him.

"You wicked man!" said the king. "I had mercy and forgave you your debt. Why didn't you have pity on your fellow servant?"

The man was speechless. The king threw him in jail.

God is like the king. He will forgive you if you ask, and he expects you to forgive others.

God's Blessing

God forgives us.

Faith to Grow

God gave us the command to love one
another. Loving others means forgiving
them. God forgives us because He loves
us. He expects us to forgive others.

Prayer

Help me to forgive others as you
forgive me. In the name of the Father,
and of the Son, and of the Holy Spirit.
Amen.

The Good Samaritan

Luke 10:25–37

A lawyer and Jesus were talking one day. The lawyer wanted to test Jesus. He said, "How am I to get eternal life?"

Jesus asked, "What do you think the law says?"

The lawyer responded, "You should love God completely, and you should love your neighbor as you love yourself."

The lawyer then asked, "Lord, who is my neighbor?"

Jesus told this story:

A man was walking down the road. Robbers jumped the man. They beat him and stole everything, even his clothes. The man lay in the road dying.

A priest came walking down the same road. He saw the man but kept walking as if the injured man were not there. Another man of religion came along. He, too, saw the man lying in the road bleeding. He crossed the road and passed by on the other side.

Later a third man came along. He was a Samaritan traveler. He saw the man who had been left to die. He stopped. He cradled the victim's head in his lap as he gave him a drink. He carefully wrapped his nearly naked body in a blanket and gently laid the man on his donkey. He took him to an inn.

The Samaritan told the innkeeper, "Take care of this man until I return. Here is money to cover the expenses. I will be returning. If his care costs more than I left you, I will repay you then."

Jesus asked the lawyer, "Who was the good neighbor?"

The lawyer answered, "The one who cared for the injured man."

Jesus said, "Go and be a good neighbor."

God's Blessing

God wants you to be a good neighbor.

Faith to Grow

Sometimes we look at people and think they are a certain way because of their looks. What Jesus tells us is that it is not what is on the outside of the person that counts. What is important is what kind of people we are on the inside, and whether we will help our neighbors.

Prayer

Lord, help me to be a good neighbor.
In the name of the Father, and
of the Son, and of the Holy Spirit.
Amen.

Jesus Teaches Us to Pray

Matthew 6:9–13; Luke 11:1–13

Jesus was praying. His disciples wanted to pray like Jesus. When he finished praying, the disciples said, "Lord, teach us how to pray."

Jesus said, "Listen, when you pray, pray like this:

"Our Father, who art in heaven, hallowed be your name; your Kingdom come; your will be done on earth as it is in heaven. Give us this day our daily bread; and forgive us our trespasses as we forgive those who trespass against us; and lead us not into temptation, but deliver us from evil. Amen."

The disciples learned this prayer and passed it on to the other believers. Jesus also said, "You must continue to pray daily." He told them a story. "A child came to his father and asked for something to eat. The loving father would not hand the child spoiled food.

He would want only the best for his son. God will hear your prayers and send the Holy Spirit to ease your mind."

The disciples found peace in praying to God and knowing that God listened as a loving father.

God's Blessing

Praying keeps us in touch with God.

Faith to Grow

Jesus wanted us to know how to pray.
He prayed often. His prayers were a
conversation with his loving father.

Prayer

Thank you for giving me the gift
of prayer. In the name of the Father,
and the Son, and the Holy Spirit,
Amen.

Jesus Blesses the Children

Mark 10:13–16

Many families gathered from far and wide to listen, learn, and be healed by Jesus. As Jesus spoke, fathers and mothers led their children to Jesus. They wanted their children to see and hear and maybe even touch the Messiah.

The disciples saw the families swarming around Jesus and shooed the families away. They said, "Can't you see that Jesus is busy?"

Jesus heard this and was disappointed with the disciples. He said, "Do not stop the children from coming to me!"

His disciples were surprised. After all, Jesus was a busy man.

Jesus opened his arms and welcomed the children. They climbed into his lap. Jesus hugged them and said, "The kingdom of heaven belongs to children. They are the ones who readily believe and are not held back by worldly things."

Placing his hands on the children and blessing them, Jesus said, "May you all be like a child, innocent and willing to believe in salvation."

God's Blessing

Jesus loves children!

Faith to Grow

Jesus loved children. Jesus saw that
adults doubted him. He knew adults
were more likely to sin than children. Jesus
wanted adults to simplify their lives
and believe as the children believed.

Prayer

Thank you for loving me, Jesus.
Help me to follow you my whole life
through. In the name of the Father,
and of the Son, and of the Holy Spirit.
Amen.

Zacchaeus

Luke 19:1–10

Zacchaeus was a wealthy man and the chief tax collector in the town of Jericho. Zacchaeus heard Jesus was coming to town. He left his desk where he was counting money and went to find Jesus.

Crowds filled the streets and Zacchaeus couldn't see over the heads of the taller people. Zacchaeus ran ahead of the crowd and climbed up into a tree. He watched as the crowd of people moved his way.

Jesus walked along the road and spoke to the crowd. When he arrived at Zacchaeus' tree, he said, "Come down and take me to your home."

"Me?" asked Zacchaeus. "You want to come to my home?" Zacchaeus scrambled down the tree. "I'm so happy! Come! We will have a feast."

The crowds grumbled and said, "Jesus is leaving us and going to a sinner's home."

Zacchaeus said to Jesus, "I give half of all I own to the poor. I repay everyone that I took too much money from when I collected taxes. To those people I give them four times as much as I took."

Jesus was pleased and said, "Today, you have been saved. I have come to seek and save the souls lost from God."

God's Blessing

Jesus welcomes everyone back to him.

Faith to Grow

Jesus loves us even if we are sinners.
He wants to bring us back to himself.

Prayer

Lord, hold me close to you.
In the name of the Father, and
of the Son, and of the Holy Spirit.
Amen.

Hosanna!

John 12:12–19

Jesus had saved the life of a man named Lazarus. Word of the miracle spread throughout the land.

Large crowds began to gather when they heard Jesus was coming to Jerusalem for Passover. The people stood in the streets waiting for Jesus to appear. They gathered palm branches as they would for a returning king. They placed their cloaks in the road, making a rainbow path for Jesus to walk on.

"Do you see him yet?" they asked each other, peering down the road. Then finally a cheer could be heard growing louder and louder. The people cried out, "Hosanna! Hosanna!"

Jesus humbly rode through the crowd on the back of a donkey colt. This was done so he could fulfill the prophecy, which said:

"Do not be afraid, city of Zion!

Here comes your king,

riding on a young donkey."

As he rode, the crowd waved palm branches and chanted, "Hosanna! Hosanna! Blessed is Jesus who comes in the name of the Lord."

The Pharisees watched the crowds and became fearful. "Look, the whole world is following him," they said to each other. "We must do something about this Jesus!"

God's Blessing

Jesus is our King.

Faith to Grow

Jesus' ride into Jerusalem is the beginning
of Holy Week. Celebrating Palm Sunday
is a way to remember Jesus' entry
into the city of Jerusalem.

Prayer

Thank you, God, for loving me so
much that you sent Jesus. In the name
of the Father, and of the Son, and
of the Holy Spirit.
Amen.

The Last Supper

Matthew 26:17–30; Luke 22:14–20

Jesus told his disciples to go to a certain room in Jerusalem where they could prepare the Passover meal. There they roasted a perfect one-year-old lamb. They made unleavened bread, and they gathered bitter herbs. Each one dressed and was ready for travel, with sandals on their feet and a walking stick in hand.

When Jesus arrived, he said, "I have looked forward to eating this Passover meal with you. When the twelve men were eating together, Jesus said, "Very soon, one of you will not treat me with the loyalty of a true friend. I am going to suffer very soon. I am telling you I will not eat again until I have completed my task and I am in the Kingdom of God."

"We would never betray you," the disciples said.

"I am sad to say that one of you will." Jesus' heart was filled with sorrow.

The disciples didn't understand what Jesus was saying.

Took

Blessed

Broke

Gave

Jesus took the bread, blessed it, broke it, and gave it to his disciples. He said, "Take and eat it; this is my body." Then he took a cup, blessed it, and gave it to them. "Drink it, all of you," he said; "this is my blood, poured out for many for the forgiveness of sins."

God's Blessing

Jesus gave up his life for our salvation.

Faith to Grow

Jesus wanted to give his disciples a way to remember him when they gathered together. We receive communion to remember Jesus.

Prayer

Thank you, God, for giving us the precious Eucharist to remember you. In the name of the Father, and of the Son, and of the Holy Spirit. Amen.

Peter Disowns Jesus

Luke 22:21–62

During the Passover meal, Jesus said, "One of you, my friends, will betray me. And, Peter, you will deny me before this night is over."

The disciples shook their heads saying, "No, Lord, we would never betray you."

Jesus said, "All of you will be tested tonight. I pray that even though you may fail, your faith will be strong and you will return and lead my people."

"I wouldn't fail you, my Lord," said Peter. "I am willing to go to prison and even lose my life for you."

Jesus said, "Tonight, you will deny knowing me three times before the rooster crows." Then Jesus led his disciples to the Mount of Olives to pray.

"Pray that you will not be tested," said Jesus. Then he went to pray by himself.

Later Jesus returned to his disciples and found them sleeping and pleaded, "Get up. You must pray."

Coming up the hillside, Jesus spotted the lights of torches coming near. They all stood and heard the growl of angry voices. Then at the head of the mob they spotted Judas followed by Roman and Jewish authorities. Judas kissed Jesus on the cheek. Two officers grabbed Jesus and arrested him. The disciples began to fight with the crowd. Peter cut off the ear of a servant.

"Stop!" said Jesus and healed the man's ear.

Bound in ropes, Jesus was taken to the High Priest. Peter followed. He waited outside the High Priest's house. A woman saw Peter and said, "You were one of Jesus' men."

Peter said, "I do not know him."

A while later someone else said, "You are Jesus' friend."

Peter said, "I don't know the man."

Later still, another man said, "You were with Jesus."

Peter again denied knowing Jesus. Then the rooster crowed. Peter realized what he had done and wept in shame.

God's Blessing

Even though he was betrayed, Jesus still forgave.

Faith to Grow

Both Judas and Peter betrayed Jesus.
The difference was that Judas didn't have
the faith in Jesus to realize that he would
be forgiven. Peter knew Jesus was
forgiving and trusted in God's mercy.

Prayer

Thank you, God, for being a forgiving and
merciful God. In the name of the Father,
and of the Son, and of the Holy Spirit.
Amen.

Jesus Is Crucified

Luke 23:1–46

Jesus was brought before the Roman governor Pilate. He was charged with misleading the people, not paying taxes to Caesar, and calling himself the Messiah.

Pilate asked, "Are you king of the Jews?"

Jesus said, "You say so."

Pilate continued to question Jesus. Finally, Pilate said, "I find this man not guilty."

The chief priest said, "This Galilean stirs up the people."

Pilate said, "Take him to Herod then. He reigns over the Galileans."

Jesus was taken to Herod. Herod was glad to see Jesus. He hoped Jesus would perform a miracle for him. But Jesus would not answer Herod's questions. Herod grew angry and sent Jesus back to Pilate.

Again Pilate found Jesus innocent and wanted to let him go. But the crowds yelled and complained. So Pilate said, "I will have him whipped."

Still the crowds yelled, "Crucify him!"

So Pilate gave up and handed Jesus over to be crucified.

Jesus was whipped. He stumbled, carrying the heavy cross on his shoulder. A soldier grabbed a man from the crowd and made him carry Jesus' cross. Crowds of people followed. Some made fun of Jesus, while others wept for him. Two criminals followed behind, carrying their crosses.

When they reached the top of the hill, Jesus was nailed to his cross.

The sky turned black. The veil of the Temple was torn down the middle, and Jesus cried out, "Father, I give you my spirit." Then Jesus died.

God's Blessing

Jesus suffered and died for our sins.

Faith to Grow

Jesus made a huge sacrifice by giving up his life to give us eternal life. He was willing to be hurt for us so that we wouldn't have to hurt.

Prayer

Thank you, Jesus, for your great sacrifice to save my soul. In the name of the Father, and of the Son, and of the Holy Spirit. Amen.

He Has Risen!

Luke 24:1–12

Mary Magdalene, Joanna, and Mary, the mother of James, went to the tomb where Jesus' body had been taken after the crucifixion. When they arrived, they saw that the stone covering the opening of the tomb had been rolled away. They looked inside. Jesus was gone. "Where is our Lord?" they said.

Suddenly, two angels appeared. The women held each other in fear.

The angels said, "Why do you look for Jesus among the dead here in this tomb? He is not here. He has been raised from the dead! Don't you remember what he told you?"

The women shook their heads.

The angel's light shone like the sun. "Jesus told you that the Son of Man would be handed over to sinners. They would crucify him, but death would not win. As foretold by the prophets, Jesus has now been raised up."

The women all agreed, "Yes! We do remember!"

Overjoyed at the good news, the three women ran back to where the disciples were staying. They burst into the room! "The Lord has risen!"

"You are beside yourselves with grief," said the disciples.

But Peter believed the women and ran to the tomb. There he saw Jesus' burial clothes lying on the floor. The tomb was empty. Peter returned to the disciples, amazed.

God's Blessing

Jesus is risen!

Faith to Grow

No more sadness! Jesus rose from
the dead just as the prophets promised.
How happy Jesus' friends were!
How blessed we are to have a loving God.

Prayer

I will rejoice in the Lord. I will rejoice
always! In the name of the Father, and
of the Son, and of the Holy Spirit.
Amen.

The Road to Emmaus

Luke 24:13–35

Two men were traveling from Jerusalem to Emmaus. As they walked down the dusty road, they talked about Jesus.

Jesus joined the two men walking. He kept himself disguised. "What are you talking about?" asked Jesus.

"Are you the only one who hasn't heard about Jesus?" they asked the stranger.

"Tell me about him," said Jesus.

The men said, "He was a prophet of God. His words were straight from God. He performed miracles and saved people's lives. Our chief priests handed Jesus over to be crucified."

"We were hoping Jesus was our Savior," agreed the two men. "Today some women from our group told us they saw angels. The angels announced, 'Jesus lives!' We don't know what to think."

Jesus said, "How foolish you are! Why are you so slow to believe what the prophets said?" Beginning with the story of Moses and on through all the prophets, Jesus reviewed the teachings. As they came into Emmaus, Jesus acted as if he were going to keep on traveling.

"It is almost dark," they said. "Stay with us."

Jesus went with them and sat down to dinner. He took the bread and said a blessing. Then he broke the bread and gave it to them.

Suddenly, their eyes were opened. "You are our Lord!"

Then Jesus vanished.

One man said, "Didn't you feel Jesus in that stranger's words? How did we not know him?" They rose from the table and quickly returned to Jerusalem to tell the others.

When they found the disciples, they said, "We have been with our Lord!"

"We, too, have news of our Lord!" said the disciples. "The Lord has been raised!

He has appeared to Simon, also!"

God's Blessing

The resurrection was a miracle from God.

Faith to Grow

Jesus walked, spoke, and ate with his
disciples so they would see and believe in
his resurrection. God's power and love
made this possible. Today we still believe.

Prayer

Lord, help me to always believe in you.
In the name of the Father, and
of the Son, and of the Holy Spirit.
Amen.

The Ascension

Matthew 28:16–20; Luke 24:49–53;

Acts 1:6–11

Jesus visited his disciples. He blessed them, saying, "You are my chosen ones. You heard all that I taught. You witnessed my ministry to the people. You must go and tell the people what you have seen and heard. Teach the people to do everything that I commanded you. Make disciples in every nation. Baptize them in the name of the Father, and of the Son, and of the Holy Spirit ... I will always be with you, even until the very end of time," said Jesus. "Wait in Jerusalem until I send the Holy Spirit to you."

The disciples watched in amazement as Jesus raised his hands and was gently taken up into heaven.

Two men dressed in white appeared beside the disciples and said, "Why are you sad at seeing Jesus leave? He will return."

The disciples journeyed back to Jerusalem, full of hope and anticipation. They were anxious to receive the

promised gift of the Holy Spirit. Their hearts were bursting with joy to share Jesus' good news of salvation.

God's Blessing

Jesus still guides us and watches over us.

Faith to Grow

Jesus was taken to heaven to sit at the right hand of his Father. He promised his people that they would not be alone.

Prayer

Thank you, Jesus, for not leaving us alone. In the name of the Father, and of the Son, and of the Holy Spirit. Amen.

The Coming of the Holy Spirit

Acts 2

Jesus' disciples gathered together daily after Jesus rose to heaven. Together they prayed and waited for the Holy Spirit whom Jesus had promised.

Suddenly one morning, a great rush of wind swirled around the room where the disciples prayed. A burst of color that looked like flames appeared and came to rest upon each one of them. Instantly, they were filled with the Holy Spirit.

The disciples fell to their knees praising God. As they prayed, they began to speak in many languages. The sound of the wind rushed through the city.

Jewish people from all over the world gathered, each hearing the disciples speaking to them in their own language. They wondered, "How do these Galileans speak every language?"

"Perhaps they have been drinking too much wine!" said a few.

Peter stood up and shouted, "These people have not been drinking! Just as the prophet Joel predicted, the

Holy Spirit has been poured out on them. Those who believe will prophesy, they will see visions, and they will dream dreams. Whoever calls on the name of the Lord will be saved."

The crowd quieted down. Peter explained, "Jesus came and served the people. He taught God's laws. He performed miracles. He was crucified and died, all with God's knowledge. Then God, the Father, raised his only Son, Jesus Christ, to sit at his right hand. Jesus promised not to forget us, and so he poured the Holy Spirit upon us. God made Jesus both Lord and Messiah."

The people's hearts were broken. They cried, "What shall we do?"

"Change your ways and be baptized," said Peter, "so that your sins may be forgiven. For God has given his promise to whomever he calls."

That day thousands accepted Jesus Christ as their Savior.

God's Blessing

The Holy Spirit lives inside us.

Faith to Grow

God didn't want to leave us alone. He gave
us the Holy Spirit to live inside each of us.
Put your hand on your heart. Do you
feel it beating? Every day, all day and all
night, your heart keeps beating. The Holy
Spirit is like your heart. He is with you
everywhere you go day and night.
He helps you to stay close to God.

Prayer

Come, Holy Spirit, and fill our souls
with your peace. In the name of
the Father, and of the Son, and
of the Holy Spirit.
Amen.

Living Christ's Way

Ephesians 6:13–18

Paul wrote a letter to a group of people called the Ephesians. Paul wanted the Ephesians to realize that God's plan was to bring all of creation together with Jesus as the Lord over all.

Paul promises that if we claim God as our Father, Jesus as our Savior, and the Holy Spirit as our guide, unity with God is possible. Paul tells us to use the following gifts—truth, righteousness, readiness, faith, and God's Word—in order to protect us from evil. He explains using these gifts as armor.

Stand ready, with truth as a belt tight around your waist, with righteousness as your breastplate, and the readiness to announce the Good News of peace as your shoes. At all times carry faith as a shield. With it you will be able to put out all the burning arrows shot by the devil. Accept your salvation as a helmet, and the Word of

God, which the Spirit gives you as your sword. Do all this in prayer, asking God's help. Pray on every occasion, as the Spirit leads.

God's Blessing

Your armor of God will protect you.

Faith to Grow

God wants us to act on the gifts of
truth, righteousness, readiness, faith,
and God's Word. If we have those gifts,
we become closer to him.

Prayer

Lord, help me to be more like you.
In the name of the Father, and
of the Son, and of the Holy Spirit.
Amen.

John's Vision of Heaven

Revelation

Jesus sent an angel to John on the island of Patmos. He wanted John to tell all Christians, "Do not be dismayed. Do not give up, even when you are being punished for believing in me. You will see your reward in heaven for your faithfulness."

John listened closely and began to write down everything the angel said. "Good and evil will fight for each and every person. God will claim the people who have lived their lives according to his laws. When Jesus returns to reclaim earth and his people, all of evil will be punished and disappear from Jesus' presence.

"Then God will make a new world. It will be beautiful. Everyone will live in peace. There will be no more crying, no more death, and no more pain. Joy in the Lord will be in the hearts of every person who is a child of God."

Then the angel said to John, "Everything I have told you is true and you can trust it. Be ready! For Jesus is going to return! He will bring great rewards to those who have been good. Jesus is the beginning and the end."

When the angel finished, John sent his writings to the seven main churches so that they would know God had not forgotten them. God's plan is happening today. Get ready!

God's Blessing

Jesus will return someday.

Faith to Grow

God made heaven a special place for his
believers. He wants us to follow his ways
so he can share heaven with us.

Prayer

God, thank you for loving me so
much. Help me to follow your ways so
I can be with you in heaven. In the
name of the Father, and of the Son,
and of the Holy Spirit.
Amen.

Let's Do This

For some extra fun, try doing these activities together. Not only are they a helpful reminder of what each story is about but they are also a great way to get all your five senses involved! Skip around or go through, story by story, it's up to you. If you'd like to read the story again before doing the activity, just look for the picture from the story, and you'll find the page number for where you can find it.

P. 8

God's Wonderful Creation
Genesis 1:1–31; 2:1–25

Materials needed: Magazines, glue or glue stick, paper or cardboard

Directions: Cut pictures of God's creations from magazines. Glue them to the paper or cardboard. Display your collage of God's creations. What do you and your family do to take care of all that God made?

Adam and Eve Disobey God
Genesis 2–3

Your parents have rules for your family. How do these rules show your parents' love for you? How do your rules keep you safe? Make a list of your family rules and decorate it with colorful designs. Hang it where everyone can see it.

P. 12

P. 16

Noah's Faithful Journey
Genesis 6—9:1–17

Materials needed: Two paper plates or cardboard, scissors, crayons, yarn or string, a paper punch

Directions: Color a rainbow on the first paper plate. Then color 6 to 8 hearts on the second paper plate. Cut out the rainbow and the hearts. Color the back side of the rainbow. Punch a hole in the center top of the rainbow and 3 to 4 holes along the bottom ends of the rainbow. On the backs of the hearts, write or draw pictures of things you can do that will please God and promises God has made to his people. (Example: God promises to love us. I obey God's rule not to steal.) Now punch a hole in each heart. Tie a string from each hole in the bottom of the rainbow to each heart. Hang your rainbow as a sign of the promises between God and his people.

God Remembers Joseph
Genesis 37–46

Materials needed: 3"x 5" cards, crayons

Directions: Write something bad that has happened to you on one side of the card. Now flip the card over and write something good that has happened as a result of the bad.

Example: We didn't get to go to the movies. / We made a cake together.

P. 24

God Watches Over Baby Moses
Exodus 2

Materials needed: Plastic berry basket and ribbon, yarn, or string

Directions: Weave the ribbon, yarn, or string through the berry basket's holes. Tie off the ends. Keep it in your room and put some of your favorite things in it as a way to remember how God kept Moses safe in his floating basket.

P. 28

God Saves the Israelites
Exodus 3–15

Be a listening detective. Spend five minutes listening to the world around you. Keep a journal and list the things you hear or draw pictures of the things you hear. Did you hear God speaking to you?

P. 32

P. 36

Crossing the Sea
Exodus 13:17—14:31

Materials needed: Vinegar, baking soda, a balloon, a small plastic bottle

Directions: Fill the plastic bottle full of vinegar. Put a tablespoon of baking soda in the balloon. Attach the mouth of the balloon securely to the mouth of the bottle. Now watch the seemingly impossible. The balloon will blow up without blowing your breath into the balloon. This is just a trick, but God doesn't need tricks. With God all things are possible.

God Provides Bread From Heaven
Exodus 16:4–35

Sit down with one of your parents and make a grocery list together. Now go over it and see if it covers all of your needs. Talk about how you forgot things, but God would never forget anything.

P. 40

P. 44

Rules to Live By
Exodus 20:1–17

Using the music from one of your favorite songs, replace the words with the Ten Commandments to help you remember them.

God Gives Samson Strength
Judges 13–16

P. 48

Materials needed: An egg, a bowl

Directions: Ask an adult if you can have an egg. Carry the egg around the kitchen or on a non-carpeted area. What would happen if you forgot to take care of the egg and dropped it? Now crack the egg in the bowl. A trusted friendship is like an egg. It is fragile and needs to be taken care of. Like trust, once the egg is broken, it can never be the same. Trusting friendships need to be protected.

P. 52

The Lord Calls Samuel
1 Samuel 3

Fill in the missing vowels, "e", "i", and "o", to decode God's message.

"L_t th_ ch_ldr_n c_m_ t_ m_."

Matthew 19:14

David and Goliath

I Samuel 17

Materials needed: Flashlight, batteries

Directions: Take the batteries out of the flashlight. Turn it on. What happens? The flashlight won't work without the batteries, which give it power. In the same way, we need God to be our source of power in order to do his work. Goliath tried to win the war on his own strength. David depended on God as his power source.

P. 56

P. 60

Solomon Asks for Wisdom

I Kings 3:5–28

Materials needed: one plain pillowcase (preferably white, but any light color will work) and permanent markers or fabric paint

Directions: Think about prayers that you would like God to hear. Decorate the pillowcase with words and pictures of your prayer requests. Let it dry. At bedtime, say the prayers you wrote down on your pillowcase.

The Lord Is my Shepherd

Psalm 23

God is like a "Safety Pin"

Ask an adult to pin a safety pin on your shirt over your heart. God's love is like that safety pin. God's love sticks to you. God's love is safe. God's love is strong. God's love holds us together. God's love shines. Put the safety pin somewhere that will remind you of just how much God loves you.

P. 68

God Knows Me

Psalm 139

Where Is God?

P. 72

Ask a friend to play this game with you.

The first person asks: "Where is God?"

The second person moves to a place and says: "Here beside me!"

The first person asks: "Where is that?"

The second person says: "Beside me in the living room."

Now move to another location in the house. Repeat the game.

What did you learn? No matter where you are, God is always with you!

Praise God!

Psalm 150

Have a Praise Jam!

Gather together as a family and bring any instruments you may have. If you don't have instruments, you can bang pot lids together for cymbals, pound on the top of a coffee can, click spoons together, fill glasses with different amounts of water and ding them with a spoon, or use whatever other instrument your imagination can invent. Now praise God for all the wonderful gifts you have in your life. Sing about it! Shout about it! Play your instruments! Make a joyful noise!

P. 76

P. 80

Isaiah the Prophet Brings Hope
Isaiah 40

Materials needed: A journal or notebook

Directions: Pray to God and talk to him about your concerns. Write down one or two of your worries. Continue to pray daily. Write down some of the things you have prayed about. As God answers your prayers, celebrate God's goodness.

Jonah and the Big Fish
Jonah 1–4

Materials needed: Basket and small ball or a ball of yarn

Directions: Place a basket on one side of a room. Then take your ball and stand far away on the opposite side of the room. Try to toss the ball into the basket. Did the ball go in the basket? How does it feel when the ball doesn't go in? What would it be like to have only one chance? God gives us many chances and helps us do his will.

P. 88

P. 100

Wise Men Visit Jesus
Matthew 2:1–18

Just like you, Jesus and his family celebrated his birthday every year. To praise the Son of God, sing "Happy Birthday" to Jesus.

Jesus in His Father's House
Luke 2:41–52

What is a church? It is God's house. Church is where you can learn about God with your family, friends, and teachers. Draw a picture of your church. Draw yourself in the community of the living church, which is the body of Christ.

P. 104

P. 112

Jesus Is Tempted
Matthew 4:1–11

Materials needed: Posterboard or paper, markers or crayons
Directions: Design a "Just say no to sin!" poster. Hang it in your room as a reminder not to sin.

Jesus Calls His Disciples
Luke 5:1–11

Play "follow the leader" with your friends. Pick a leader and follow that person everywhere, doing everything he or she does for the next 15 minutes. It might be fun at first, but the longer you play the game, the more difficult it becomes. The disciples followed Jesus until his death. At first it was exciting. Then the closer it got to his crucifixion, the harder it was. But they were dedicated to Jesus and continued to do his work even after his death and resurrection.

P. 116

P. 120

Why Worry?
Matthew 6:25–34

Write down or draw a picture of something that you are worried about. Tell God, "I am not going to worry about that anymore because I know you will take care of me." Now tear up that piece of paper and throw it in the trash.

Jairus' Daughter
Mark 5:21–43

Ask an adult to give you a lima bean seed. Is it dead or alive? Wrap the lima bean in a damp paper towel, and put it inside a sealable plastic bag. Tape the bag to a sunny window. Watch the lima bean come to life. All life comes from God, and he is our source of hope. Even though we were once dead in sin, Jesus made us alive again in him.

P. 128

P. 132

Jesus Feeds 5,000
Matthew 14:13–21

Materials needed: Paper, scissors, pencil

Directions: Fold your paper like a fan, making each section about three inches wide. Draw a three-inch wide fish. Leave part of the fish's tail on the fold and part of its mouth on the opposite fold. Now cut out the fish, making sure to leave the tail and mouth on the folds. Unfold your fish cutout. One fish is now many fish!

The Lost and Found Sheep
Matthew 18:12–24

P. 144

Materials needed: 100 pennies

Directions: Ask your mom, dad, or another adult to hide one of your 100 pennies in a room. Now go on a treasure hunt to find it. After all, 100 pennies equal a whole dollar, but 99 pennies cannot be exchanged for that one-dollar bill. When you find the lost penny, celebrate! God also celebrates every time one of his lost children is found.

To Forgive or Not to Forgive
Matthew 18:21–35

P. 148

The next time you eat chocolate pudding, notice how much pudding is left in the dish after you finish. Did you scrape and scrape with your spoon to get every last bite? Some was still left over, wasn't it. Now ask an adult if you can wash the dish by yourself. If you're not old enough yet, watch someone else wash the dish. See how a little soap and water cleans it right up? No matter how well behaved we are, we're like that dirty pudding dish. But God's forgiveness washes us clean of our sins. When someone hurts your feelings, think about that pudding and practice God's forgiveness.

The Good Samaritan
Luke 10:25–37

Materials needed: A box, pretty wrapping paper, a stone, a brown grocery bag, tape, scissors

P. 152

Directions: Wrap up the stone in the box. Ask your mom, dad, or another adult what they think will be inside. Now open the box. Talk about how the outside packaging didn't match what was on the inside.

P. 160

Jesus Blesses the Children
Mark 10.13–16

Materials needed: paper, crayons or markers, pen

Directions: Make a "God's Blessings" journal. First, stack a few sheets of paper and fold them in half. Decorate the front of the journal by drawing pictures that make you think of God. Now every day or every week, write down the blessings that God has given you. It will help you to see how he is always working in your life.

Zacchaeus
Luke 19:1–10

Materials needed: a soiled shirt, spot remover (such as Shout or Oxy-Clean), a washing machine

P. 164

Directions: Look for one of your shirts that you've spilled food on. Ask an adult to apply spot remover. Watch the stain disappear. Then wash and dry the shirt in the washing machine as usual. Jesus still loves us even though we are stained, just like that shirt. When we become children of God, he washes the stains away.

The Last Supper
Luke 22:14–20

Materials needed: An empty chair and an extra place setting at the dinner table

Directions: Every night for a week when you gather for dinner, set a place for Jesus at your table to remember him. This is also a good opportunity to talk about what it's like to miss a friend or loved one.

P. 172

Jesus Is Crucified
Luke 23:1–46

Materials needed: Large stick, small stick, string

Directions: Hold the two sticks together perpendicular to each other, making a cross. Tie the sticks together with your string by weaving the string over and under each branch of the cross, until it is sturdy. Hang it where it will remind you of God's great sacrifice for you.

P. 180

He Is Risen!
Luke 24:1–2

Have a family celebration. Go around the table and have each family member say one thing they are grateful for. Continue doing this until everyone has had at least one turn.

P. 184

The Road to Emmaus
Luke 24:13–35

With permission, remove the shade from a lamp and look at the bulb when the light is off. Turn the switch on. The bulb lights up when the power is turned on. God was the power in Jesus' life. He is the power in our lives, too. His light shines on!

P. 188

P. 200

Living Christ's Way
Ephesians 6:13–18

Materials needed: Tin foil, cardboard, tape

Directions: Cut the cardboard into the shape of a shield. Wrap tin foil around the shield and secure with tape. Think about how this shield would protect a warrior. God's gifts will protect you in the same way. For more armor gear, check out the scripture passage.

John's Vision of Heaven
Revelation

Draw a picture of what you think heaven will be like. Now talk about what each person in your family thinks. God's heaven will be all that you talked about and even more!

P. 204

Let's Talk About This

Would you like to talk about the stories some more? Check out this list. Talking is a great way to learn from each other, and can lead to some very meaningful times together. Skip around or go through topic by topic, it's up to you. If you'd like to read the story again, just look for the picture from the story, and you'll find the page number for where you can find it.

P. 20

God's Promise to Abraham
Genesis 12:1–8; 18:10–12; 21:1–7

How do you think it might feel to leave everyone and everything you know? Did Abraham have to go alone? Who is always with you, even when you feel alone?

God Feeds Hungry Elijah
1 Kings 17:1–16

What kinds of things do you have that you could share with your community? You could gather toys to give to a shelter or earn money to give to a charity. Another idea might be to volunteer at a soup kitchen or gather cans of food for a food drive.

P. 64

P. 84

God Keeps Daniel Safe
Daniel 6:1–25

Have you ever been frightened by a thunderstorm? Thunder and lightning sound and look scary. What do you do when it thunders? You probably run inside your house to stay safe. That's how God protects us. Run to God and pray when you are frightened.

The Annunciation
Luke 1:26–38

P. 92

God asks us to be his servants. When we take care of each other, we are serving each other and following God's commands to love one another. Look around you and see where God is asking you to serve.

P. 96

The Birth of Christ
Luke 2:1–20

What do you think Jesus did every day when he was your age? What things did Jesus do that you do, too? We don't know for sure, but he probably skinned his knees, played outside, and got hugs and kisses from his mom, just like you.

The Baptism of Jesus
Matthew 3:1–17

P. 108

When you were a baby, you joined together with members of your family and the church, and you were baptized. You became part of God's family. Your baptismal record and photograph are visible proofs of your baptism. When you were baptized, the priest poured holy water over your head and anointed you with oil. You were dressed in white clothes as a sign of being washed clean of sin. How did your family celebrate your baptism?

The Faith of the Centurion
Matthew 8:5–13

P. 124

During Mass, right before Communion, we express our simple faith in Jesus, just like the centurion did. Even though we're not worthy, we tell the Lord, "Only say the word and I will be healed." We believe that if we ask for God's mercy, he will heal us of our sins. Listen in church for the people to speak the words of the centurion. Remember, Jesus was pleased with the faith of the centurion.

"I am the Bread of Life"
John 6:22–70

P. 136

Just like your stomach gets hungry, your soul gets hungry, too. So how can you feed your soul? You feed your soul with God's life-giving words in the Bible. We hear God's words during mass when the Gospel is read. We also feed our souls by sharing the body and blood of Jesus when we receive Communion.

You Are the Son of God
Matthew 16:13–20

P. 140

Peter was not perfect, but he believed in Jesus. Jesus gave Peter the responsibility to carry on the church after Jesus died and ascended to heaven. We are not perfect either, and we too have been chosen by Jesus to become present-day saints. How does it feel to be chosen by Jesus? What can you do to show your thankfulness to him?

P. 156

Jesus Teaches Us to Pray
Matthew 6:9–13; Luke 11:1–4

Prayer is like talking with your family. God our Father loves you and wants to hear you talk to him. What can you pray about right now?

The Ascension
Matthew 28:16–20; Luke 24:49–53

Gather your family and talk about what being a family means. How do you help each other? How do you spend time together? How are God and Jesus part of a family? How are they part of your family?

P. 192

P. 176

Peter Disowns Jesus
Luke 22:21– 63

Forgiving others is very difficult, especially when they've hurt you. Who do you need to forgive? Is there someone you need to ask for forgiveness?

The Coming of the Holy Spirit
Acts 2:1–47

Put your hand on your heart. Do you feel it beating? Every day, all day, and all night, your heart keeps beating. The Holy Spirit is like your heart. He is with you everywhere you go day and night. He helps you to stay close to God.

P. 196